Instant Vortex Cookbook 2021

100 Easy To Make Instant Vortex Recipes For Beginners

Zoe Baker

© **Copyright 2021 - All rights reserved.**

The content contained within this book may not be reproduced, duplicated or transmitted without direct written permission from the author or the publisher.

Under no circumstances will any blame or legal responsibility be held against the publisher, or author, for any damages, reparation, or monetary loss due to the information contained within this book. Either directly or indirectly.

Legal Notice:

This book is copyright protected. This book is only for personal use. You cannot amend, distribute, sell, use, quote or paraphrase any part, or the content within this book, without the consent of the author or publisher.

Disclaimer Notice:

Please note the information contained within this document is for educational and entertainment purposes only. All effort has been executed to present accurate, up to date, and reliable, complete information. No warranties of any kind are declared or implied. Readers acknowledge that the author is not engaging in the rendering of legal, financial, medical or professional advice. The content within this book has been derived from various sources. Please consult a licensed professional before attempting any techniques outlined in this book.

By reading this document, the reader agrees that under no circumstances is the author responsible for any losses, direct or indirect, which are incurred as a result of the use of information contained within this document, including, but not limited to, — errors, omissions, or inaccuracies.

Table of Content

BREAKFAST	9
Herbed Breakfast Eggs	10
Eggs in Zucchini Nests	11
Breakfast Liver Pate	12
Keto Bread-Free Breakfast Sandwich	13
Egg Butter	14
Awesome Lemon Bell Peppers	15
Avocado Rolls	16
Portobello Hearty Mushroom Burgers	17
Crazy Mac and Cheese	18
Zucchini Noodles with Avocado Sauce	19
Candied Walnut and Strawberry	20
Blueberry Spelt Pancakes	21
Good Morning Energy Crackers	22
Masala Quinoa Meal	23
SNACK	24
Squid Rings	25
Carrot Chips	26
Corn Okra Bites	27
Salty Potato Chips	28
Corn & Beans Fries	29
Sugary Apple Fritters	30
Oregano Onion Rings	31
Cinnamon Mixed Nuts	32
Apple & Cinnamon Chips	33
Sesame Cabbage & Prawns Egg Roll Wraps	34
Rosemary Potatoes	35
Crunchy Mozzarella Sticks with Sweet Thai Sauce	36
Chili Cheese Crisps	37
Parmesan Baked Tomatoes	38

Gingered Scallops 39
Baked Bacon Potatoes 40
Coconut Shrimps 41
Guacamole Tortilla Chips 42
Roasted Chickpeas 43
Supreme French Fries 44
Butter Cashews 45
Cinnamon Banana Chips 46
Perfect Cinnamon Toast 47
Easy Baked Chocolate Mug Cake 48
Angel Food Cake 49
Fried Peaches 50

LUNCH 51

Zucchini Hassel back 52
Butternut Squash Hash 53
Butter Mushrooms with Chives 54
Fennel & Spinach Quiche 55
Lemony Baby Potatoes 56
White Mushrooms with Snow Peas 57
Gold Potatoes and Bell Pepper Mix 58
Potato with Bell Peppers 59
Chinese Long Beans Mix 60
Portobello Mushrooms with Spinach 61
Summer Squash Mix 62
Corn with Tomatoes Salad 63
Colored Veggie Mix 64
Minty Leeks Medley 65
Corn and Tomatoes 66
Soft Tofu with Veggies 67
Oregano Bell Peppers 68
Yellow Lentils Herbed Mix 69

Creamy Zucchini and Sweet Potatoes	70
Meaty Egg Rolls	71
Ham Hash	72
Pork Fried Rice	73
Ketogenic Mac & Cheese	74
Salmon Pie	75
Garlic Chicken Stir	77
Chicken Stew	78
Goulash	79
Beef & broccoli	80
Ground Beef Mash	81
Chicken Casserole	82
Chicken Hash	83
DINNER	84
Air Fryer Chicken Kabobs	85
Chicken Fried Rice in Air Fryer	86
Air Fried Chicken Tikkas	87
Nashville Hot Chicken in Air Fryer	89
Air Fryer Panko Breaded Chicken Parmesan	91
Air Fryer Rosemary Turkey	92
Air Fryer Lamb Chops	93
Air Fried Shrimp and Sauce	94
Air Fryer Italian Meatball	95
Air Fryer Coconut Milk Chicken	96
Air Fryer Cauliflower Rice	97
Buttery Cod	98
Creamy Chicken	99
Mushroom and Turkey Stew	100
Basil Chicken	101
Eggplant Bake	102
Meatball Casserole	103

Herbed Lamb Rack	104
Baked Beef	105
Old-Fashioned Pork Chops	106
Turkey Pillows	107
Chicken Wings	108
Chicken Cordon Bleu	109
Fried Chicken	110
Sesame Chicken	111
Chicken and Potatoes	112
Polish Sausage and Sourdough Kabobs	113
Ranch Meatloaf with Peppers	114
Indian Beef Samosas	115

BREAKFAST

Herbed Breakfast Eggs

Intermediate Recipe Preparation Time: 10 minutes
Cooking Time: 17 minutes **Serving:** 2

INGREDIENTS:

- 4 eggs
- 1 teaspoon oregano
- 1 teaspoon parsley, dried
- ½ teaspoon sea salt
- 1 tablespoon chives, chopped
- 1 tablespoon cream
- 1 teaspoon paprika

DIRECTIONS:

1. Place the eggs in the air fryer basket and cook them for 17-minutes at 320°Fahrenheit. Meanwhile, combine the parsley, oregano, cream, and salt in shallow bowl. Chop the chives and add them to cream mixture. When the eggs are cooked, place them in cold water and allow them to chill. After this, peel the eggs and cut them into halves. Remove the egg yolks and add yolks to cream mixture and mash to blend well with a fork. Then fill the egg whites with the cream-egg yolk mixture. Serve immediately.

NUTRITION: Calories 136 Fat 9.3g Carbs 2.1g Protein 11.4g

Eggs in Zucchini Nests

Basic Recipe

Preparation Time: 10 minutes **Cooking Time:** 7 minutes **Serving:** 2

INGREDIENTS:

- 4 teaspoons butter
- ½ teaspoon paprika
- ½ teaspoon black pepper
- ¼ teaspoon sea salt
- 4-ounces cheddar cheese, shredded
- 4 eggs
- 8-ounces zucchini, grated

DIRECTIONS:

1. Grate the zucchini and place the butter in ramekins. Add the grated zucchini in ramekins in the shape of nests. Sprinkle the zucchini nests with salt, pepper, and paprika. Beat the eggs and pour over zucchini nests.
2. Top egg mixture with shredded cheddar cheese. Preheat the air fryer basket and cook the dish for 7-minutes. When the zucchini nests are cooked, chill them for 3-minutes and serve them in the ramekins.

NUTRITION: Calories 221 Fat 17.7g Carbs 2.9g Protein 13.4g

Breakfast Liver Pate

Intermediate Recipe Preparation Time: 5 minutes **Cooking Time:** 10 minutes **Serving:** 7 **INGREDIENTS:**

- 1 lb. chicken liver
- 1 teaspoon salt
- ½ teaspoon cilantro, dried
- 1 yellow onion, diced
- 1 teaspoon ground black pepper
- 1 cup water
- 4 tablespoons butter

DIRECTIONS:

1. Chop the chicken liver roughly and place it in the air fryer basket tray. Add water to air fryer basket tray and add diced onion. Preheat your air fryer to 360°Fahrenheit and cook chicken liver for 10- minutes. Dry out the chicken liver when it is finished cooking.
2. Transfer the chicken liver to blender, add butter, ground black pepper and dried cilantro and blend. Once you get a pate texture, transfer to liver pate bowl and serve immediately or keep in the fridge for later.

NUTRITION: Calories 173 Fat 10.8g Carbs 2.2g Protein 16.1g

Keto Bread-Free Breakfast Sandwich

Intermediate Recipe Preparation Time: 10 minutes **Cooking Time:** 10 minutes **Serving:** 2

INGREDIENTS:

- 6-ounces ground chicken
- 2 slices of cheddar cheese
- 2 lettuce leaves
- 1 tablespoon dill, dried
- ½ teaspoon sea salt
- 1 egg
- 1 teaspoon cayenne pepper
- 1 teaspoon tomato puree

DIRECTIONS:

1. Combine the ground chicken with the pepper and sea salt. Add the dried dill and stir. Beat the egg into the ground chicken mixture. Make 2 medium- sized burgers from the ground chicken mixture. Preheat your air fryer to 380°Fahrenheit. Spray the air fryer basket tray with olive oil and place the ground chicken burgers inside of it. Cook the chicken burgers for 10-minutes Flip over burgers and cook for an additional 6-minutes. When the burgers are cooked, transfer them to the lettuce leaves. Sprinkle the top of them with tomato puree and with a slice of cheddar cheese. Serve immediately!

NUTRITION: Calories 324 Fat 19.2g Carbs 2.3g Protein 34.8g

Egg Butter

Basic Recipe

Preparation Time: 5 minutes **Cooking Time:** 17 minutes **Serving:** 2 **INGREDIENTS:**

- 4 eggs
- 4 tablespoons butter
- 1 teaspoon salt

DIRECTIONS:

1. Cover the air fryer basket with foil and place the eggs there. Transfer the air fryer basket into the air fryer and cook the eggs for 17 minutes at 320°Fahrenheit. When the time is over, remove the eggs from the air fryer basket and put them in cold water to chill them. After this, peel the eggs and chop them up finely. Combine the chopped eggs with butter and add salt. Mix it until you get the spread texture. Serve the egg butter with the keto almond bread.

NUTRITION: Calories 164 Fat 8.5g Carbs 2.67g Protein 3g

Awesome Lemon Bell Peppers

Intermediate Recipe Preparation Time: 10 minutes **Cooking Time:** 5 minutes **Serving:** 4

INGREDIENTS:

- 4 bell peppers
- 1 teaspoon olive oil
- 1 tablespoon lemon juice
- 1/4 teaspoon garlic, minced
- 1 teaspoon parsley, chopped
- 1 pinch sea salt
- Pinch of pepper

DIRECTIONS:

1. Preheat your Air Fryer to 390 degrees F in —AIR FRY! mode
2. Add bell pepper in the Air fryer
3. Drizzle with it with the olive oil and air fry for 5 minutes
4. Take a serving plate and transfer it
5. Take a small bowl and add garlic, parsley, lemon juice, salt, and pepper
6. Mix them well and Drizzle with the mixture over the peppers
7. Serve and enjoy!

NUTRITION: Calories 59 kcal Carbs 6g Fat 4g Protein 2g

Avocado Rolls

Intermediate Recipe

Preparation Time: 10 minutes **Cooking Time:** 25 minutes **Serving:** 4

INGREDIENTS:

- 10 Dr. Sebi friendly wrappers
- 3 avocados, sliced
- 1 tomato, diced
- Salt and pepper to taste
- 1 tablespoon olive oil
- 4 tablespoon peppers
- 2 tablespoons date sugar
- 1 tablespoon hemp seed oil
- 1 tablespoon alkaline vinegar

DIRECTIONS:

1. Take a bowl and mash avocados
2. Stir in tomatoes, salt, and pepper, mix well
3. Arrange wrappers and scoop mix on top
4. Roll and seal edges
5. Cook in your Air fryer for 5 minutes at 350 degrees F
6. Take a bowl and mix remaining ingredients, serve with sauce
7. Enjoy!

NUTRITION: Calories 422 kcal Carbs 38 g Fat 15 g

Portobello Hearty Mushroom Burgers

Intermediate Recipe Preparation Time: 10 minutes **Cooking Time:** 20 minutes **Serving:** 4

INGREDIENTS:

- 2 cups Portobello mushroom caps
- 1 avocado, sliced
- 1 plum tomato, sliced
- 1 cup torn lettuce
- 1 cup purslane
- 1/2 teaspoon cayenne
- 1 teaspoon oregano
- 2 teaspoons basil
- 3 tablespoons olive oil

DIRECTIONS:

1. Remove mushroom stems and cut off ½ inch slices from top slice
2. Take a bowl and mix in onion powder, cayenne, oregano, olive oil, and basil
3. Cover Air Fryer basket with a baking sheet, brush grape seed oil
4. Put caps on baking sheet
5. Pour mixture on top and let them sit for 10 minutes
6. Preheat your Air Fryer 400 degrees F and transfer to Fryer, bake it for 8 minutes, flip and Bake it for 8 minutes more
7. Lay caps on serving dish, layer sliced avocado, tomato, lettuce, purslane
8. Cover with another mushroom cap
9. Serve and enjoy!

NUTRITION: Calories 358 kcal Carbs 49 g Fat 13 g Protein 15g

Crazy Mac and Cheese

Intermediate Recipe Preparation Time: 10 minutes
Cooking Time: 20 minutes **Serving:** 4

INGREDIENTS:

- 12 ounces alkaline pasta
- 1/4 cup chickpea flour
- 1 cup raw Brazilnut
- 1/2 teaspoon onion powder
- 1 teaspoon salt
- 2 teaspoons grape seed oil
- 1 cup hemp seed milk
- 1 cup of water
- 1/2 key lime, juiced

DIRECTIONS:

1. Take a bowl and add nuts, soak overnight. Cook pasta according to package Preheat your Air Fryer to 325 degrees F. Transfer cooked pasta to a baking dish and Drizzle with oil, add remaining ingredients to a blender and blend until smooth
2. Pour mix over mac and mix
3. Transfer to Air Fryer and Bake it for 25 minutes
4. Serve and enjoy!

NUTRITION: Calories 255 kcal Carbs 1 g Fat 23 g Protein 12 g

Zucchini Noodles with Avocado Sauce

Basic Recipe

Preparation Time: 10 minutes **Cooking Time:** 15 minutes **Serving:** 4

INGREDIENTS:

- 3 medium zucchinis
- 1 and 1/2 cup cherry tomatoes
- 1 avocado
- 2 green onions, sliced
- 1 garlic clove
- 3 tablespoons olive oil
- Juice of 1 key lemon
- 1 tablespoon spring water
- Salt and cayenne to taste

DIRECTIONS:

1. Preheat your Air Fryer to 385 degrees F
2. Take your Air Fryer cooking basket and cover with parchment paper
3. Put tomatoes and Drizzle with olive oil, season with salt and cayenne
4. Transfer to your Fryer and cook for 10-15 minutes until starting to split
5. Add quartered avocado, parsley, sliced green onion, garlic, spring water, lemon juice, 1/2 teaspoon salt to a food processor
6. Blend until creamy
7. Cut zucchini ends using use spiralizer to turn into zoodles
8. Mix zoodles with sauce
9. Divide into 3 bowls and serve with tomatoes
10. Enjoy!

NUTRITION: Calories 180 kcal Carbs 14 g Fat 14 g Protein 2g

Candied Walnut and Strawberry

Intermediate Recipe Preparation Time: 10 minutes **Cooking Time:** 10 minutes **Serving:** 4

INGREDIENTS:

- 1/2 cup walnuts, chopped
- 1 tablespoon raw agave nectar
- 1/4 teaspoon salt
- Dressing
- 1/2 cup strawberries, sliced
- 2 tablespoons shallots
- 1/2 cup grape seed oil
- 2 teaspoons raw agave nectar
- 1 and 1/2 teaspoon lime juice
- 1 teaspoon onion powder
- 1/2 teaspoon ginger
- 1/4 teaspoon dill
- 1/4 teaspoon salt

DIRECTIONS:

1. Coat walnuts with agave and salt
2. Transfer to a cooking basket lined with parchment
3. Preheat your Air Fryer to 300 degrees F roast for 6- 8 minuteslet them cool. Add dressing ingredients to a bowl, blend for half a minute
4. Add walnuts. Mix and enjoy!

NUTRITION: Calories 260 kcal Carbs 28 g Fat 16 g Protein 4g

Blueberry Spelt Pancakes

Intermediate Recipe Preparation Time: 10 minutes **Cooking Time:** 10 minutes **Serving:** 4

INGREDIENTS:

- 2 cups spelt flour
- 1 cup hemp milk
- 1/2 cup spring water
- 2 tablespoons grape seed
- 1/2 cup Agave
- 1/2 cup blueberries
- 1/4 teaspoon Sea Moss
- 2 tablespoons Hemp Seeds
- Grape seed oil

DIRECTIONS:

1. Place Moss, agave, hemp seeds, grape seed oil, spelt in a large bowl
2. Mix well
3. Add milk and water, mix until you have your desired consistency
4. Toss in blueberries and toss well
5. Preheat your Air Fryer to 325 degrees F
6. Transfer batter to Air Fryer basket lined with parchment paper
7. Cook for 3-4 minutes, flip and cook for 3 minutes more until golden on both side
8. Serve and enjoy!

NUTRITION: Calories 276 kcal Carbs 36 g Fat 11 g Protein 9g

Good Morning Energy Crackers

Intermediate Recipe Preparation Time: 10 minutes **Cooking Time:** 25 minutes **Serving:** 4

INGREDIENTS:

- 1/2 cup hemp seeds
- 1/2 cup quinoa
- 1/2 cup sunflower seeds
- 1/2 cup sesame seeds
- 1 garlic clove, crushed
- 1/2 teaspoon cayenne pepper
- Salt and pepper to taste
- 1 and 1/4 cup spring water

DIRECTIONS:

1. Preheat your oven to 280 degrees F
2. Take a bowl and mix everything, spread the mix in your cooking basket lined with baking sheet
3. Bake it for 20-25 minutes
4. Break into pieces and serve
5. Enjoy!

NUTRITION: Calories 148 kcal Carbs 1.4 g Fat 1.6 g Protein 4.8g

Masala Quinoa Meal

Intermediate Recipe Preparation Time: 10 minutes **Cooking Time:** 45 minutes **Serving:** 4

INGREDIENTS:

- 1/2 white onion, chopped
- Pinch of salt
- 1 red bell pepper, chopped
- 1/2 jalapeno pepper, seeded and chopped
- 2 tablespoons ginger, peeled and grated
- 1 tablespoon masala powder
- 1 cup quinoa
- 2 cups Sebi friendly vegetable stock
- 1/2 lemon, juiced

DIRECTIONS:

1. Preheat your Air Fryer to 350 degrees F
2. Take a large skillet and place it over medium heat, add onion and salt, Sauté for 3 minutes
3. Add pepper, jalapeno, ginger, garam masala and Sauté for 1 minute
4. Add quinoa to the stock, stir
5. Transfer mix to Air Fryer cooking basket
6. Cook for about 3-40 minutes until fluffy
7. Add lemon juice and fluff more
8. Adjust the seasoning accordingly and serve
9. Enjoy!

NUTRITION: Calories 503 kcal Carbs 103 g Fat 3 g Protein 32g

SNACK

Squid Rings

Basic Recipe

Preparation Time: 10 minutes **Cooking Time:** 4 minutes **Servings:** 2 **INGREDIENTS:**

- 2 squid tubes
- 2 eggs
- 1/3 cup flour
- ¼ teaspoon salt
- ½ teaspoon onion powder
- ½ teaspoon garlic powder

DIRECTIONS:

1. Wash and peel the squid cubes carefully. Then slice the squid cubes into the rings.
2. Beat the eggs in the bowl and whisk them.
3. Then dip the squid rings in the whisked eggs.
4. Combine together flour, salt, onion powder, and garlic powder. Stir the mixture with the help of the fork.
5. Then coat the squid rings with the flour mixture.
6. Preheat the air fryer to 400 F.
7. Put the squid rings onto the air fryer rack.
8. Cook the squid rings for 4 minutes.
9. Shake the squid rings after 3 minutes of cooking.
10. When the squid rings are cooked – let them chill till the room temperature
11. Enjoy!

NUTRITION: Calories 383 Fat 10.5 Carbs 17.2 Protein 55.8

Carrot Chips

Basic Recipe

Preparation Time: 10 minutes **Cooking Time:** 20 minutes **Servings:** 2 **INGREDIENTS:**

- 3 carrots
- ½ teaspoon salt
- ½ teaspoon ground black pepper
- 1 tablespoon canola oil

DIRECTIONS:

1. Peel the carrot and slice into the chips.
2. Then sprinkle the uncooked carrot chips with the salt, ground black pepper, and canola oil.
3. Shake the carrot chips carefully.
4. Preheat the air fryer to 360 F.
5. Put the carrot chips in the air fryer basket.
6. Shake the carrot chips in halfway.
7. Check the doneness of the carrot chips while cooking.
8. Chill the carrot chips and serve.
9. Enjoy!

NUTRITION: Calories 101 Fat 7 Carbs 9.3 Protein 0.8

Corn Okra Bites

Basic Recipe

Preparation Time: 10 minutes **Cooking Time**: 4 minutes **Servings:** 2 **INGREDIENTS:**

- 4 tablespoon corn flakes, crushed
- 9 oz okra
- 1 egg
- ½ teaspoon salt
- 1 teaspoon olive oil

DIRECTIONS:

1. Preheat the air fryer to 400 F.
2. Chop the okra roughly.
3. Combine together the corn flakes and salt.
4. Crack the egg into the bowl and whisk it.
5. Toss the chopped okra in the whisked egg.
6. Then coat the chopped okra with the corn flakes.
7. Put the chopped okra in the air fryer basket and sprinkle with the olive oil.
8. Cook the okra for 4 minutes
9. Shake the okra after 2 minutes of cooking.
10. When the okra is cooked – let it chill gently.
11. Enjoy!

NUTRITION: Calories 115 Fat 4.8 Carbs 12.7 Protein 5.2

Salty Potato Chips

Basic Recipe

Preparation Time: 10 minutes **Cooking Time**: 19 minutes **Servings:** 2 **INGREDIENTS:**

- 3 potatoes
- 1 tablespoon canola oil
- ½ teaspoon salt

DIRECTIONS:

1. Wash the potatoes carefully and do not peel them. Slice the potatoes into the chips.
2. Sprinkle the potato chips with the olive oil and salt. Mix the potatoes carefully.
3. Preheat the air fryer to 400 F. Put the potato chips in the air fryer basket and cook for 19 minutes
4. Shake the potato chips every 3 minutes
5. When the potato chips are cooked – chill them well.
6. Enjoy!

NUTRITION: Calories 282 Fat 7.3 Carbs 50.2 Protein 5.4

Corn & Beans Fries

Basic Recipe

Preparation Time: 10 minutes **Cooking Time:** 10 minutes **Servings:** 2 **INGREDIENTS:**

- ¼ cup corn flakes crumbs
- 1 egg
- 10 oz green beans
- 1 tablespoon canola oil
- ½ teaspoon salt
- 1 teaspoon garlic powder

DIRECTIONS:

1. Preheat the air fryer to 400 F.
2. Put the green beans in the bowl.
3. Beat the egg in the green beans and stir carefully until homogenous.
4. Then sprinkle the green beans with the salt and garlic powder.
5. Shake gently.
6. Then coat the green beans in the corn flakes crumbs well.
7. Put the green beans in the air fryer basket in one layer.
8. Cook the green beans for 7 minutes
9. Shake the green beans twice during the cooking.
10. When the green beans are cooked – let them chill and serve.
11. Enjoy!

NUTRITION: Calories 182 Fat 9.4 Carbs 21 Protein 6.3

Sugary Apple Fritters

Basic Recipe

Preparation Time: 10 minutes **Cooking Time:** 10 minutes **Servings:** 2 **INGREDIENTS:**

- 2 red apples
- 1 teaspoon sugar
- 1 tablespoon flour
- 1 tablespoon semolina
- 1 teaspoon lemon juice
- ½ teaspoon ground cinnamon
- 1 teaspoon butter
- 1 egg

DIRECTIONS:

1. Peel the apples and grate them.
2. Sprinkle the grated apples with the lemon juice.
3. Then add sugar, flour, semolina, and ground cinnamon.
4. Mix the mixture and crack the egg.
5. Mix the apple mixture carefully.
6. Preheat the air fryer to 370 F.
7. Toss the butter in the air fryer basket and melt it.
8. When the butter is melted – make the medium fritters from the apple mixture. Use 2 spoons for this step.
9. Place the fritters in the air fryer basket and cook for 6 minutes
10. After this, flip the fritters to another side and cook for 2 minutes more.
11. Dry the cooked fritters with the help of the paper towel and serve.
12. Enjoy!

NUTRITION: Calories 207 Fat 4.6 Carbs 40.3 Protein 4.5

Oregano Onion Rings

Basic Recipe

Preparation Time: 14 minutes **Cooking Time:** 10 minutes **Servings:** 2 **INGREDIENTS:**

- 1 tablespoon oregano
- 1 tablespoon flour
- ½ teaspoon cornstarch
- 1 egg
- ½ teaspoon salt
- 2 white onions, peeled
- 1 tablespoon olive oil

DIRECTIONS:

1. Crack the egg into the bowl and whisk it. Combine together the flour and cornstarch in the separate bowl.
2. Add oregano and salt. Shake the mixture gently. Peel the onions and slice them to get the —rings‖.
3. Then dip the onion rings in the whisked egg. After this, coat the onion rings in the flour mixture.
4. Preheat the air fryer to 365 F.
5. Spray the air fryer basket with the olive oil inside. Then place the onion rings in the air fryer and cook for 8 minutes
6. Shake the onion rings after 4 minutes of cooking. Let the cooked meal chill gently.
7. Serve it!

NUTRITION: Calories 159 Fat 9.6 Carbs 15.5 Protein 4.6

Cinnamon Mixed Nuts

Basic Recipe

Preparation Time: 5 minutes **Cooking Time:** 20 minutes **Servings**: 5 **INGREDIENTS:**

- ½ cup pecans
- ½ cup walnuts
- ½ cup almonds
- A pinch of cayenne pepper
- 2 tbsp sugar
- 2 tbsp egg whites
- 2 tsp cinnamon

DIRECTIONS

1. Add the pepper, sugar, and cinnamon to a bowl and mix them well; set aside. In another bowl, mix in the pecans, walnuts, almonds, and egg whites. Add the spice mixture to the nuts and give it a good mix. Lightly grease the frying basket with cooking spray. Pour in the nuts, and cook them for 10 minutes on Air Fry function at 350 F. Stir the nuts using a wooden vessel, and cook for further for 10 minutes Pour the nuts in the bowl. Let cool.

NUTRITION: Calories 180 Fat 12g Carbs 13g Protein 6g

Apple & Cinnamon Chips

Basic Recipe

Preparation Time: 15 minutes **Cooking Time:** 10 minutes **Servings:** 2 **INGREDIENTS:**

- 1 tsp sugar
- 1 tsp salt
- 1 whole apple, sliced
- ½ tsp cinnamon
- Confectioners' sugar for serving

DIRECTIONS:

2. Preheat your Air Fryer to 400 F. In a bowl, mix cinnamon, salt and sugar; add the apple slices. Place the prepared apple spices in the cooking basket and cook for 10 minutes on Bake function. Dust with sugar and serve.

NUTRITION: Calories 110 Fat 0g Carbs 27g Protein 1g

Sesame Cabbage & Prawns Egg Roll Wraps

Basic Recipe

Preparation Time: 32 minutes **Cooking Time**: 18 minutes **Servings**: 4 **INGREDIENTS:**

- 2 tbsp vegetable oil
- 1-inch piece fresh ginger, grated
- 1 tbsp minced garlic
- 1 carrot, cut into strips
- ¼ cup chicken broth
- 2 tbsp reduced-sodium soy sauce
- 1 tbsp sugar
- 1 cup shredded Napa cabbage
- 1 tbsp sesame oil
- 8 cooked prawns, minced
- 1 egg
- 8 egg roll wrappers

DIRECTIONS

3. In a skillet over high heat, heat vegetable oil, and cook ginger and garlic for 40 seconds, until fragrant. Stir in carrot and cook for another 2 minutes Pour in chicken broth, soy sauce, and sugar and bring to a boil.
4. Add cabbage and let simmer until softened, for 4 minutes Remove skillet from the heat and stir in

sesame oil. Let cool for 15 minutes Strain cabbage mixture, and fold in minced prawns. Whisk an egg in a small bowl. Fill each egg roll wrapper with prawn mixture, arranging the mixture just below the center of the wrapper.

5. Fold the bottom part over the filling and tuck under. Fold in both sides and tightly roll up. Use the whisked egg to seal the wrapper. Place the rolls into a greased frying basket, spray with oil and cook for 12 minutes at 370 F on Air Fry function, turning once halfway through.

NUTRITION: Calories 149.3 Fat 3.5g Carbs 20g Protein 8.8 g

Rosemary Potatoes

Basic Recipe

Preparation Time: 10 minutes **Cooking Time:** 25 minutes **Servings:** 2 **INGREDIENTS:**

- 1.5 pounds potatoes, halved
- 2 tbsp olive oil
- 3 garlic cloves, grated
- 1 tbsp minced fresh rosemary
- 1 tsp salt
- ¼ tsp freshly ground black pepper

DIRECTIONS:

6. In a bowl, mix potatoes, olive oil, garlic, rosemary, salt, and pepper, until they are well-coated. Arrange the potatoes in the basket and cook t 360 F on Air Fry function for 25 minutes, shaking twice during the cooking. Cook until crispy on the outside and tender on the inside.

NUTRITION: Calories 132 Fats: 2.5g Carbs 18.3g Protein 9.5g

Crunchy Mozzarella Sticks with Sweet Thai Sauce

Intermediate Recipe Preparation Time: 2 hours
Cooking Time: 20 minutes **Servings:** 2
INGREDIENTS:

- 12 mozzarella string cheese
- 2 cups breadcrumbs
- 3 eggs
- 1 cup sweet Thai sauce
- 4 tbsp skimmed milk

DIRECTIONS

7. Pour the crumbs in a bowl. Crack the eggs into another bowl and beat with the milk. One after the other, dip each cheese sticks in the egg mixture, in the crumbs, then egg mixture again and then in the crumbs again.
8. Place the coated cheese sticks on a cookie sheet and freeze for 1 to 2 hours. Preheat Air Fry function to
380 F. Arrange the sticks in the frying basket without overcrowding. Cook for 8 minutes, flipping

them halfway through cooking to brown evenly. Cook in batches. Serve with a sweet Thai sauce.

NUTRITION: Calories 173 Fat 5.6g Carbs 27g Protein 3.3g

Chili Cheese Crisps

Basic Recipe

Preparation Time: 17 minutes **Cooking Time:** 10 minutes **Servings**: 3 **INGREDIENTS:**

- 4 tbsp grated cheese + extra for rolling
- 1 cup flour + extra for kneading
- ¼ tsp chili powder
- ½ tsp baking powder
- 3 tsp butter
- A pinch of salt

DIRECTIONS

9. In a bowl, mix in the cheese, flour, baking powder, chili powder, butter, and salt. The mixture should be crusty. Add some drops of water and mix well to get dough. Remove the dough on a flat surface.
10. Rub some extra flour in your palms and on the surface, and knead the dough for a while. Using a rolling pin, roll the dough out into a thin sheet.
11. With a pastry cutter, cut the dough into your desired lings' shape. Add the cheese lings to the basket, and cook for 8 minutes at 350 F on Air Fry function, flipping once halfway through.

NUTRITION: Calories 1085 Fat 71g Carbs 64g Protein 55g

Parmesan Baked Tomatoes

Basic Recipe

Preparation Time: 10 minutes **Cooking Time:** 10 minutes **Servings:** 4 **INGREDIENTS:**

- 1 cup grated mozzarella cheese
- 1 cup grated Parmesan cheese
- ½ cup chopped basil
- Olive oil
- 4 tomatoes, halved

DIRECTIONS:

12. Grease a baking pan with some cooking spray. Place tomato halves over the pan; stuff with cheese and basil.
13. Place Instant Vortex over the kitchen platform. Arrange to drip pan in the lower position. Press
    —Bake, set timer to 10 minutes, and set the temperature to 400°F.
14. When Instant Vortex is pre-heated, it will display
    —Add Food on its screen. Open the door, and take out the middle roasting tray.
15. Place the pan over the tray and push it back; close door and cooking will start. Midway, it will display
    —Turn Food on its screen; ignore it, and it will continue to cook after 10 seconds. Cook until cheese is bubbly.
16. Open the door after the cooking cycle is over; serve warm.

NUTRITION: Calories 486 Fat 7.5g Carbs 11g Protein 17.5g

Gingered Scallops

Basic Recipe

Preparation Time: 10 minutes **Cooking Time:** 15 minutes **Servings:** 4-6 **INGREDIENTS:**

- 6 very large sea scallops
- ¼ cup tamarind sauce
- 1 tablespoon dark brown sugar
- 6 slices bacon, cut in half crosswise
- 1 ½ teaspoon minced ginger

DIRECTIONS:

17. In a mixing bowl, add tamarind sauce, brown sugar, ginger, and scallops. Combine the ingredients to mix well with each other. Set aside for 15-20 minutes
18. Then, wrap each scallop with two bacon slices. Secure using toothpicks.
19. Grease a baking pan with some cooking spray. Place scallops over the pan.
20. Place the air fryer over the kitchen platform. Arrange to drip pan in the lower position. Press
—Air Fry,‖ set the timer to 15 minutes, and set the temperature to 350°F.
21. When the air fryer is pre-heated, it will display —Add Food‖ on its screen. Open the door, and take out the middle roasting tray.
22. Place the pan over the tray and push it back; close door and cooking will start. Midway, it will display
—Turn Food‖ on its screen; flip scallops and close door. Cook until bacon is crispy and brown.
23. Open the door after the cooking cycle is over; serve warm.

NUTRITION: Calories 173 Fat 14g Carbs 3g Protein 5.5g

Baked Bacon Potatoes

Basic Recipe

Preparation Time: 5 minutes **Cooking Time:** 10 minutes **Servings:** 4 **INGREDIENTS:**

- ¼ cup chopped scallions
- 1 cup grated cheddar cheese
- 3 russet potatoes, cleaned and cut into 1-inch rounds
- ¼ cup butter
- 3 tablespoon bacon bits, cooked and crumbled

DIRECTIONS:

24. Grease a baking pan with some cooking spray. Place potato over the pan; brush with butter and top with scallions and cheese.
25. Place Instant Vortex over the kitchen platform. Arrange to drip pan in the lower position. Press

    ―Bake,‖ set timer to 15 minutes, and set the temperature to 400°F. Instant Vortex will start pre- heating.
26. When Instant Vortex is pre-heated, it will display

    ―Add Food‖ on its screen. Open the door, and take out the middle roasting tray.
27. Place the pan over the tray and push it back; close door and cooking will start. Midway, it will display

    ―Turn Food‖ on its screen; ignore it, and it will continue to cook after 10 seconds. Cook until cheese is bubbly.
28. Open the door after the cooking cycle is over; serve warm with bacon on top.

NUTRITION: Calories 330 Fat 12g Carbs 48g Protein 7.5g

Coconut Shrimps

Basic Recipe

Preparation Time: 10 minutes **Cooking Time:** 12 minutes **Servings:** 4 **INGREDIENTS:**

- 8 ounces coconut milk
- ½ cup panko breadcrumbs
- 8 large shrimp, peeled and deveined
- Salt and ground black pepper, to taste
- ½ teaspoon cayenne pepper

DIRECTIONS:

29. In a mixing bowl, add salt, black pepper, and coconut milk. Combine the ingredients to mix well with each other.
30. In another bowl, add breadcrumbs, cayenne pepper, Ground black pepper, and salt. Combine the ingredients to mix well with each other. Coat the shrimps evenly with first coconut mixture and then with crumbs. Grease a baking pan with some cooking spray. Place shrimps over the pan.
31. Place Instant Vortex over the kitchen platform. Arrange to drip pan in the lower position. Press —Air Fry,‖ set the timer to 15 minutes, and set the temperature to 350°F.
32. When air Fryer is pre-heated, it will display —Add Food‖ on its screen. Open the door, and take out the middle roasting tray. Place the pan over the tray and push it back; close door and cooking will start. Midway, it will display —Turn Food‖ on its screen; flip shrimps and close door.
33. Open the door after the cooking cycle is over; serve warm.

NUTRITION: Calories 209 Fat 15g Carbs 6g Protein 4.5g

Guacamole Tortilla Chips

Basic Recipe

Preparation Time: 10 minutes **Cooking Time:** 15 minutes **Servings:** 4 **INGREDIENTS:**

- Chips:
- 1 tablespoon cumin powder
- 1 tablespoon paprika powder
- 12 corn tortillas
- 2 tablespoon olive oil
- Ground black pepper and salt to taste
- Guacamole:
- 1 small firm tomato, chopped
- 1 large avocado, pitted, peeled and mashed
- A pinch dried parsley

DIRECTIONS:

1. In a mixing bowl, add all chips ingredients. Combine the ingredients to mix well with each other. In another bowl, add guacamole ingredients. Combine the ingredients to mix well with each other.
2. Place Instant Vortex over the kitchen platform. Arrange to drip pan in the lower position.
3. Press —Air Fry,| set the timer to 15 minutes, and set the temperature to 375°F.
4. In the rotisserie basket, add chips mixture.
5. When the air fryer is pre-heated, it will display —Add Food| on its screen. Open the door and lock the basket. Press the red lever and arrange the basket on the left side; now, just simply rest the basket rod over the right side.
6. Close door and press —Rotate|; cooking will start. Cook until chips are evenly golden.
7. Open the door after the cooking cycle is over; serve chips with guacamole.

NUTRITION: Calories 140 Fat 13g Carbs 11g Protein 2.5g

Roasted Chickpeas

Intermediate Recipe Preparation Time: 10 minutes
Cooking Time: 45 minutes **Servings:** 2
INGREDIENTS:
- 1 (15 ounces) can chickpeas, Dry outed
- 1/4 teaspoon garlic powder
- 1/4 teaspoon ground cumin
- 1/4 teaspoon ground coriander
- 1/4 teaspoon curry powder
- 1/8 teaspoon salt
- 1/4 teaspoon chili pepper powder
- 1/4 teaspoon paprika
- Olive oil

DIRECTIONS:
1. In a mixing bowl, add chickpeas and spices. Combine the ingredients to mix well with each other.
2. Place Instant Vortex over the kitchen platform. Arrange to drip pan in the lower position.
3. Press —Air Fry,‖ set the timer to 35 minutes, and set the temperature to 375°F.
4. In the rotisserie basket, add chickpea mixture.
5. When the air fryer is pre-heated, it will display —Add Food‖ on its screen. Open the door and lock the basket. Press the red lever and arrange the basket on the left side; now, just simply rest the basket rod over the right side.
6. Close door and press —Rotate‖; cooking will start. Cook until evenly toasted and golden brown. Cook for 5-10 minutes more if needed. Open the door after the cooking cycle is over; serve warm

NUTRITION: Calories 132 Fat 13g Carbs 11g Protein 2.4g

Supreme French Fries

Basic Recipe

Preparation Time: 10 minutes **Cooking Time:** 10 minutes **Servings:** 2 **INGREDIENTS:**

- ½ teaspoon onion powder
- ½ teaspoon garlic powder
- 1-pound potatoes, peeled and cut into strips
- 3 tablespoons olive oil
- 1 teaspoon paprika
- Salt to taste (optional)

DIRECTIONS:

7. In a mixing bowl, add potato strips and water. Soak for an hour; Dry out and dry pieces completely over paper towels.
8. In a mixing bowl, add a strip and other ingredients. Combine the ingredients to mix well with each other.
9. Place Instant Vortex over the kitchen platform. Arrange to drip pan in the lower position.
10. Press —Air Fry,‖ set the timer to 30 minutes, and set the temperature to 375°F. Instant Vortex will start pre-heating.
11. In the rotisserie basket, add potato mix.
12. When Instant Vortex is pre-heated, it will display —Add Food‖ on its screen. Open the door and lock the basket. Press the red lever and arrange the basket on the left side; now, just simply rest the basket rod over the right side.
13. Close door and press —Rotate‖; cooking will start.
14. Open the door after the cooking cycle is over; serve warm.

NUTRITION: Calories 176 Fat 11g Carbs 17g Protein 3g

Butter Cashews

Basic Recipe

Preparation Time: 5 minutes **Cooking Time:** 5 minutes **Servings:** 5-6 **INGREDIENTS:**

- 1 teaspoon butter, melted
- 1 ½ cups raw cashew nut
- Salt and black pepper to taste

DIRECTIONS:

15. In a mixing bowl, add cashews and other ingredients. Combine the ingredients to mix well with each other.
16. Grease a baking tray with some cooking spray. Place cashews over the tray.
17. Place Instant Vortex over the kitchen platform. Arrange to drip pan in the lower position.
18. Press —Air Fry,‖ set timer to 5 minutes, and set the temperature to 355°F.
19. When the air fryer is pre-heated, it will display —Add Food‖ on its screen. Open the door, and take out the middle roasting tray.
20. Place the baking tray over the roasting tray and push it back; close door and cooking will start. Midway it will display —Turn Food‖ on its screen; shake baking tray and close door.
21. Open the door after the cooking cycle is over; serve warm.

NUTRITION: Calories 233 Fat 15g Carbs 12g Protein 6g

Cinnamon Banana Chips

Basic Recipe

Preparation Time: 10 minutes **Cooking Time**: 6 minutes **Servings:** 4 **INGREDIENTS:**

- ¼ teaspoon cocoa powder
- A pinch of cinnamon powder
- 5 large firm bananas, peeled

DIRECTIONS:

22. Slice bananas thinly in a horizontal manner and combine with cocoa and cinnamon in a bowl.
23. Place Instant Vortex over the kitchen platform. Arrange to drip pan in the lower position.
24. Press —Air Fry,‖ set timer to 7 minutes, and set the temperature to 380°F.
25. When the air fryer is pre-heated, it will display —Add Food‖ on its screen. Open the door, and take out the middle roasting tray.
26. Place slices (cook in batches if needed) over the tray and push it back; close door and cooking will start. Midway, it will display —Turn Food‖ on its screen; ignore it, and it will continue to cook after 10 seconds. Cook until the slices crisps.
27. Open the door after the cooking cycle is over; serve warm.

NUTRITION: Calories 173 Fat 0.5g Carbs 34g Protein 2.5g

Perfect Cinnamon Toast

Basic Recipe

Preparation Time: 10 minutes **Cooking Time:** 5 minutes **Servings:** 6 **INGREDIENTS:**

- 2 tsp. pepper
- 1 ½ tsp. vanilla extract
- 1 ½ tsp. cinnamon
- ½ C. sweetener of choice
- 1 C. coconut oil
- 12 slices whole wheat bread

DIRECTIONS:

28. Melt coconut oil and mix with sweetener until dissolved. Mix in remaining ingredients minus bread till incorporated.
29. Spread mixture onto bread, covering all area.
30. Pour the coated pieces of bread into the Oven rack/basket. Place the Rack on the middle-shelf of the Air fryer oven. Set temperature to 400°F, and set time to 5 minutes
31. Remove and cut diagonally. Enjoy!

NUTRITION: Calories 124 Fat 2g Carbs 12g Protein 0g

Easy Baked Chocolate Mug Cake

Basic Recipe

Preparation Time: 5 minutes **Cooking Time:** 10 minutes **Servings**: 3 **INGREDIENTS:**

- ½ cup cocoa powder
- ½ cup stevia powder
- 1 cup coconut cream
- 1 package cream cheese, room temperature
- 1 tablespoon vanilla extract
- 1 tablespoons butter

DIRECTIONS:

1. Preheat the air fryer oven for 5 minutes
2. In a mixing bowl, combine all ingredients.
3. Use a hand mixer to mix everything until fluffy.
4. Pour into greased mugs.
5. Place the mugs in the fryer basket.
6. Bake it for 15 minutes at 350°F.
7. Place in the fridge to chill before serving. **NUTRITION:** Calories 744 Fat 69.7g Protein 13.9g Carbs: 4g

Angel Food Cake

Basic Recipe

Preparation Time: 5 minutes **Cooking Time**: 30 minutes **Servings**: 12 **INGREDIENTS:**

- ¼ cup butter, melted
- 1 cup powdered erythritol
- 1 teaspoon strawberry extract
- 12 egg whites
- 2 teaspoons cream of tartar
- A pinch of salt

DIRECTIONS:

1. Preheat the air fryer oven for 5 minutes
2. Mix the egg whites and cream of tartar.
3. Use a hand mixer and whisk until white and fluffy.
4. Add the rest of the ingredients except for the butter and whisk for another minute.
5. Pour into a baking dish.
6. Place in the air fryer basket and cook for 30 minutes at 400°F or if a toothpick inserted in the middle comes out clean.
7. Drizzle with melted butter once cooled.

NUTRITION: Calories 65 Fat 5g Carbs: 1g Protein 3.1g

Fried Peaches

Intermediate Recipe

Preparation Time: 2 hours 10 minutes
Cooking Time: 15 minutes **Servings:** 4
INGREDIENTS:

- 4 ripe peaches (1/2 a peach = 1 serving)
- 1 1/2 cups flour
- Salt
- 2 egg yolks
- 3/4 cups cold water
- 1 1/2 tablespoons olive oil
- 2 tablespoons brandy
- 4 egg whites
- Cinnamon/sugar mix

DIRECTIONS:

1. Mix flour, egg yolks, and salt in a mixing bowl. Slowly mix in water, then add brandy. Set the mixture aside for 2 hours and go do something for 1 hour 45 minutes
2. Boil a large pot of water and cut and X at the bottom of each peach. While the water boils fill another large bowl with water and ice. Boil each peach for about a minute, then plunge it in the ice bath. Now the peels should basically fall off the peach. Beat the egg whites and mix into the batter mix. Dip each peach in the mix to coat.
3. Pour the coated peach into the Oven rack/basket. Place the Rack on the middle-shelf of the Air fryer oven. Set temperature to 360°F, and set time to 10 minutes
4. Prepare a plate with cinnamon/sugar mix, roll peaches in mix and serve.

NUTRITION: Calories 306 Fat 3g Protein 10g Carbs: 2.7g

LUNCH

Zucchini Hassel back

Basic Recipe

Preparation Time: 15 minutes **Cooking Time:** 12 minutes **Servings:** 2 **INGREDIENTS:**

- 1 zucchini
- 4 oz. Cheddar, sliced
- ½ teaspoon salt
- ½ teaspoon dried oregano
- ½ teaspoon ground coriander
- ½ teaspoon paprika
- 3 tablespoons heavy cream
- 1 teaspoon olive oil
- ¼ teaspoon minced garlic

DIRECTIONS:

1. Cut the zucchini into a Hassel back shape.
2. Then fill the zucchini with the sliced cheese.
3. Coat the zucchini Hassel back with salt, dried oregano, ground coriander, paprika, minced garlic, olive oil, and heavy cream.
4. Preheat the air fryer to 400 F.
5. Wrap the zucchini Hassel back in foil and place in the preheated air fryer.
6. Cook for 12 minutes
7. When the zucchini is cooked, remove it from the foil and cut into 2 pieces.

NUTRITION: Calories 215 Fat 14.9 Carbs 5.7 Protein 15.6

Butternut Squash Hash

Basic Recipe

Preparation Time: 10 minutes **Cooking Time:** 14 minutes **Servings:** 4 **INGREDIENTS:**

- 1 cup chicken stock
- 10 oz. butternut squash
- 1 teaspoon salt
- 1 tablespoon butter
- 1 teaspoon dried dill
- ¼ teaspoon paprika

DIRECTIONS:

1. Peel the butternut squash and chop it.
2. Preheat the air fryer to 370 F.
3. Pour the chicken stock into the air fryer basket tray.
4. Add salt, chopped butternut squash, butter, dried dill, and paprika.
5. Stir gently.
6. Cook for 14 minutes
7. Transfer to a bowl.
8. Use a fork to mash.
9. Serve immediately.

NUTRITION: Calories 61 Fat 3.3 Carbs 6.2 Protein 0.9

Butter Mushrooms with Chives

Basic Recipe

Preparation Time: 10 minutes **Cooking Time:** 10 minutes **Servings:** 2 **INGREDIENTS:**

- 1 cup white mushrooms
- 4 oz chive stems
- 1 tablespoon butter
- 1 teaspoon olive oil
- 1 teaspoon dried rosemary
- 1/3 teaspoon salt
- ¼ teaspoon ground nutmeg

DIRECTIONS:

1. Preheat the air fryer to 400 F.
2. Pour the olive oil and butter in the air fryer basket tray.
3. Add dried rosemary, salt, and ground nutmeg.
4. Stir gently.
5. Dice the chives.
6. Add the diced chives in the air fryer basket tray.
7. Cook for 5 minutes
8. Meanwhile, chop the white mushrooms.
9. Add the mushrooms.
10. Stir the mixture and cook it for a further 5 minutes at the same temperature.
11. Stir then serve.

NUTRITION: Calories 104 Fat 8.4 Carbs 6.8 Protein 1.8

Fennel & Spinach Quiche

Basic Recipe

Preparation Time: 15 minutes
Cooking Time: 10 minutes

Servings: 5

INGREDIENTS:

- 10 oz. fennel, chopped
- 1 cup spinach
- 5 eggs
- ½ cup almond flour
- 1 teaspoon olive oil
- 1 tablespoon butter
- 1 teaspoon salt
- ¼ cup heavy cream
- 1 teaspoon ground black pepper

DIRECTIONS:

1. Chop the spinach and combine it with the chopped fennel in a large bowl.
2. Crack the egg in a separate bowl and whisk.
3. Combine the whisked eggs with the almond flour, butter, salt, heavy cream, and ground black pepper.
4. Whisk together to mix
5. Preheat the air fryer to 360 F.
6. Grease the air fryer basket tray with the olive oil.
7. Add both mixtures.
8. Cook the quiche for 18 minutes
9. Let the quiche cool.
10. Remove it from the air fryer and slice into servings.

NUTRITION: Calories 209 Fat 16.1 Carbs 7.4 Protein 8.3

Lemony Baby Potatoes

Basic Recipe

Preparation Time: 10 minutes **Cooking Time:** 25 minutes **Servings:** 6 **INGREDIENTS:**

- 2 tablespoons olive oil
- 2 springs rosemary, chopped
- 2 tablespoons parsley, chopped
- 2 tablespoons oregano, chopped
- Salt and black pepper to the taste
- 1 tablespoon lemon rind, grated
- 3 garlic cloves, minced
- 2 tablespoons lemon juice
- 2 pounds baby potatoes

DIRECTIONS:

1. In a bowl, mix baby potatoes with oil, rosemary, parsley, oregano, salt, pepper, lemon rind, garlic and lemon juice, toss, transfer potatoes to your air fryer's basket and cook at 356 degrees F for 25 minutes
2. Divide potatoes between plates and serve as a side dish.
3. Enjoy!

NUTRITION: Calories 204 Fat 4 Carbs 17 Protein 6

White Mushrooms with Snow Peas

Basic Recipe
Preparation Time: 10 minutes **Cooking Time:** 15 minutes **Servings:** 2 **INGREDIENTS:**

- Salt and black pepper to the taste
- 7 ounces snow peas
- 8 ounces white mushrooms, halved
- 1 yellow onion, cut into rings
- 2 tablespoons coconut aminos
- 1 teaspoon olive oil

DIRECTIONS:
1. In a bowl, snow peas with mushrooms, onion, aminos, oil, salt and pepper, toss well, transfer to a pan that fits your air fryer, introduce in the fryer and cook at 350 degrees F for 15 minutes. Divide between plates and serve as a side dish. Enjoy!

NUTRITION: Calories 175 Fat 4 Carbs 12 Protein 7

Gold Potatoes and Bell Pepper Mix

Basic Recipe

Preparation Time: 10 minutes **Cooking Time:** 25 minutes **Servings:** 4 **INGREDIENTS:**

- 4 gold potatoes, cubed
- 1 yellow onion, chopped
- 2 teaspoons olive oil
- 1 green bell pepper, chopped
- Salt and black pepper to the taste
- ½ teaspoon thyme, dried

DIRECTIONS:

2. Heat up your air fryer at 350 degrees F, add oil, heat it up, add onion, bell pepper, salt and pepper, stir and cook for 5 minutes
3. Add potatoes and thyme, stir, cover and cook at 360 degrees F for 20 minutes
4. Divide between plates and serve as a side dish.
5. Enjoy!

NUTRITION: Calories 201 Fat 4 Carbs 12 Protein 7

Potato with Bell Peppers

Basic Recipe

Preparation Time: 10 minutes **Cooking Time:** 25 minutes **Servings:** 6 **INGREDIENTS:**

- 6 ounces jarred roasted red bell peppers, chopped
- 3 garlic cloves, minced
- 2 tablespoons parsley, chopped
- Salt and black pepper to the taste
- 2 tablespoons chives, chopped
- 4 potatoes, peeled and cut into wedges
- Cooking spray

DIRECTIONS:

1. In a pan that fits your air fryer, combine roasted bell peppers with garlic, parsley, salt, pepper, chives, potato wedges and the oil, toss, transfer to your air fryer and cook at 350 degrees F for 25 minutes
2. Divide between plates and serve as a side dish.
3. Enjoy!

NUTRITION: Calories 212 Fat 6 Carbs 11 Protein 5

Chinese Long Beans Mix

Basic Recipe

Preparation Time: 10 minutes **Cooking Time:** 10 minutes **Servings:** 4 **INGREDIENTS:**

- ½ teaspoon coconut aminos
- 1 tablespoon olive oil
- A pinch of salt and black pepper
- 4 garlic cloves, minced
- 4 long beans, trimmed and sliced

DIRECTIONS:

4. In a pan that fits your air fryer, combine long beans with oil, aminos, salt, pepper and garlic, toss, introduce in your air fryer and cook at 350 degrees F for 10 minutes
5. Divide between plates and serve as a side dish.
6. Enjoy!

NUTRITION: Calories 170 Fat 3 Carbs 7 Protein 3

Portobello Mushrooms with Spinach

Basic Recipe

Preparation Time: 10 minutes **Cooking Time:** 12 minutes **Servings:** 4 **INGREDIENTS:**

- 4 big Portobello mushroom caps
- 1 tablespoon olive oil
- 1 cup spinach, torn
- 1/3 cup vegan breadcrumbs
- ¼ teaspoon rosemary, chopped

DIRECTIONS:

1. Rub mushrooms caps with the oil, place them in your air fryer's basket and cook them at 350 degrees F for 2 minutes
2. Meanwhile, in a bowl, mix spinach, rosemary and breadcrumbs and stir well.
3. Stuff mushrooms with this mix, place them in your air fryer's basket again and cook at 350 degrees F for 10 minutes
4. Divide them between plates and serve as a side dish.
5. Enjoy!

NUTRITION: Calories 152 Fat 4 Carbs 9 Protein 5

Summer Squash Mix

Basic Recipe

Preparation Time: 10 minutes **Cooking Time:** 10 minutes **Servings:** 4 **INGREDIENTS:**

- 3 ounces coconut cream
- ½ teaspoon oregano, dried
- Salt and black pepper
- 1 big yellow summer squash, peeled and cubed
- 1/3 cup carrot, cubed
- 2 tablespoons olive oil

DIRECTIONS:

1. In a pan that fits your air fryer, combine squash with carrot, oil, oregano, salt, pepper and coconut cream, toss, transfer to your air fryer and cook at 400 degrees F for 10 minutes
2. Divide between plates and serve as a side dish.
3. Enjoy!

NUTRITION: Calories 170 Fat 4 Carbs 8 Protein 6

Corn with Tomatoes Salad

Basic Recipe

Preparation Time: 10 minutes **Cooking Time:** 10 minutes **Servings:** 4 **INGREDIENTS:**

- 3 cups corn
- A Drizzle with of olive oil
- Salt and black pepper to the taste
- 1 teaspoon sweet paprika
- 1 tablespoon stevia
- ½ teaspoon garlic powder
- ½ iceberg lettuce head, cut into medium strips
- ½ romaine lettuce head, cut into medium strips
- 1 cup canned black beans, Dry outed
- 3 tablespoons cilantro, chopped
- 4 green onions, chopped
- 12 cherry tomatoes, sliced

DIRECTIONS:

1. Put the corn in a pan that fits your air fryer, Drizzle with the oil, add salt, pepper, paprika, stevia and garlic powder, introduce in your air fryer and cook at 350 degrees F for 10 minutes
2. Transfer corn to a salad bowl, add lettuce, black beans, tomatoes, green onions and cilantro, toss, divide between plates and serve as a side salad.
3. Enjoy!

NUTRITION: Calories 162 Fat 6 Carbs 7 Protein 6

Colored Veggie Mix

Basic Recipe

Preparation Time: 10 minutes **Cooking Time:** 12 minutes **Servings:** 6 **INGREDIENTS:**

- 1 zucchini, sliced in half and roughly chopped
- 1 orange bell pepper, roughly chopped
- 1 green bell pepper, roughly chopped
- 1 red onion, roughly chopped
- 4 ounces brown mushrooms, halved
- Salt and black pepper to the taste
- 1 teaspoon Italian seasoning
- 1 cup cherry tomatoes, halved
- ½ cup kalamata olives, pitted and halved
- ¼ cup olive oil
- 3 tablespoons balsamic vinegar
- 2 tablespoons basil, chopped

DIRECTIONS:

1. In a bowl, mix zucchini with mushrooms, orange bell pepper, green bell pepper, red onion, salt, pepper, Italian seasoning and oil, toss well, transfer to preheated air fryer at 380 degrees F and cook them for 12 minutes
2. In a large bowl, combine mixed veggies with tomatoes, olives, vinegar and basil, toss, divide between plates and serve cold as a side dish.
3. Enjoy!

NUTRITION: Calories 180 Fat 5 Carbs 10 Protein 6

Minty Leeks Medley

Basic Recipe

Preparation Time: 10 minutes **Cooking Time:** 12 minutes **Servings:** 4 **INGREDIENTS:**

- 6 leeks, roughly chopped
- 1 tablespoon cumin, ground
- 1 tablespoon mint, chopped
- 1 tablespoon parsley, chopped
- 1 teaspoon garlic, minced
- A Drizzle with of olive oil
- Salt and black pepper to the taste

DIRECTIONS:

1. In a pan that fits your air fryer, combine leeks with cumin, mint, parsley, garlic, salt, pepper and the oil, toss, introduce in your air fryer and cook at 350 degrees F for 12 minutes
2. Divide Minty Leeks Medley between plates and serve as a side dish.
3. Enjoy!

NUTRITION: Calories 131 Fat 7 Carbs 10 Protein 6

Corn and Tomatoes

Basic Recipe

Preparation Time: 10 minutes **Cooking Time:** 13 minutes **Servings:** 4 **INGREDIENTS:**

- 2 cups corn
- 4 tomatoes, roughly chopped
- 1 tablespoon olive oil
- Salt and black pepper to the taste
- 1 tablespoon oregano, chopped
- 1 tablespoon parsley, chopped
- 2 tablespoons soft tofu, pressed and crumbled

DIRECTIONS:

1. In a pan that fits your air fryer, combine corn with tomatoes, oil, salt, pepper, oregano and parsley, toss, introduce the pan in your air fryer and cook at 320 degrees F for 10 minutes
2. Add tofu, toss, introduce in the fryer for 3 minutes more, divide between plates and serve as a side dish.
3. Enjoy!

NUTRITION: Calories 171 Fat 7 Carbs 9 Protein 6

Soft Tofu with Veggies

Basic Recipe
Preparation Time: 10 minutes **Cooking Time:** 14 minutes **Servings:** 2 **INGREDIENTS:**
- 1 broccoli head, florets separated and steamed
- 1 tomato, chopped
- 3 carrots, chopped and steamed
- 2 ounces soft tofu, crumbled
- 1 teaspoon parsley, chopped
- 1 teaspoon thyme, chopped
- Salt and black pepper to the taste

DIRECTIONS:
4. In a pan that fits your air fryer, combine broccoli with tomato, carrots, thyme, parsley, salt and pepper, toss, introduce the fryer and cook at 350 degrees F for 10 minutes
5. Add tofu, toss, introduce in the fryer for 4 minutes more, divide between plates and serve as a side dish.
6. Enjoy!

NUTRITION: Calories 174 Fat 4 Carbs 12 Protein 3

Oregano Bell Peppers

Basic Recipe

Preparation Time: 10 minutes **Cooking Time:** 15 minutes **Servings:** 4 **INGREDIENTS:**

- 1 tablespoon olive oil
- 1 sweet onion, chopped
- 1 red bell pepper, chopped
- 1 orange bell pepper, chopped
- 1 green bell pepper, chopped
- Salt and black pepper to the taste
- ½ cup cashew cheese, shredded
- 1 tablespoon oregano, chopped

DIRECTIONS:

7. In a pan that fits your air fryer, combine onion with red bell pepper, green bell pepper, orange bell pepper, salt, pepper, oregano and oil, toss, introduce in the fryer and cook at 320 degrees F for 10 minutes
8. Add cashew cheese, toss, introduce in the fryer for 4 minutes more, divide between plates and serve as a side dish.
9. Enjoy!

NUTRITION: Calories 172 Fat 4 Carbs 8 Protein 7

Yellow Lentils Herbed Mix

Basic Recipe

Preparation Time: 10 minutes **Cooking Time:** 20 minutes **Servings:** 4 **INGREDIENTS:**

- 1 cup yellow lentils soaked in water for 1 hour and dry outed
- 1 hot chili pepper, chopped
- 1-inch ginger piece, grated
- ½ teaspoon turmeric powder
- 1 teaspoon garam masala
- Salt and black pepper to the taste
- 2 teaspoons olive oil
- ½ cup cilantro, chopped
- 1 and ½ cup spinach, chopped
- 4 garlic cloves, minced
- ¾ cup red onion, chopped

DIRECTIONS:

1. In a pan that fits your air fryer, mix lentils with chili pepper, ginger, turmeric, garam masala, salt, pepper, olive oil, cilantro, spinach, onion and garlic, toss, introduce in your air fryer and cook at 400 degrees F for 15 minutes
2. Divide lentils mix between plates and serve as a side dish.
3. Enjoy!

NUTRITION: Calories 202 Fat 2 Carbs 12 Protein 4

Creamy Zucchini and Sweet Potatoes

Basic Recipe

Preparation Time: 10 minutes **Cooking Time:** 16 minutes **Servings:** 8 **INGREDIENTS:**

- 1 cup veggie stock
- 2 tablespoons olive oil
- 2 sweet potatoes, peeled and cut into medium wedges
- 8 zucchinis, cut into medium wedges
- 2 yellow onions, chopped
- 1 cup coconut milk
- Salt and black pepper to the taste
- 1 tablespoon coconut aminos
- ¼ teaspoon thyme, dried
- ¼ teaspoon rosemary, dried
- 4 tablespoons dill, chopped
- ½ teaspoon basil, chopped

DIRECTIONS:

1. Heat up a pan that fits your air fryer with the oil over medium heat, add onion, stir and cook for 2 minutes
2. Add zucchinis, thyme, rosemary, basil, potato, salt, pepper, stock, milk, aminos and dill, stir, introduce in your air fryer, cook at 360 degrees F for 14 minutes, divide between plates and serve as a side dish.
3. Enjoy!

NUTRITION: Calories 133 Fat 3 Carbs 10 Protein 5

Meaty Egg Rolls

Basic Recipe

Preparation Time: 5 minutes **Cooking Time:** 20 minutes **Servings:** 4

INGREDIENTS:

- ½ Cup almond flour
- 1 teaspoon sea salt, fine
- ¼ cup water
- 7 ounces ground beef
- 1 egg
- 1 teaspoon paprika
- 1 teaspoon black pepper
- 1 tablespoon olive oil

DIRECTIONS:

1. Preheat your water until it boils, and then get out your almond flour and sea salt. Mix it in a bowl.
2. Add in your boiling water, and mix well. Knead into a soft dough, and then set it to the side.
3. Combine your ground beef, black pepper and paprika, mixing well.
4. Roast your meat for five minutes on medium heat, stirring frequently using a saucepan. Beat your egg in.
5. Cook your ground beef for four minutes, and then roll the dough out. Cut it into six squares.
6. Put your ground beef in each square, and then roll them into sticks.
7. Sprinkle with olive oil, and preheat your air fryer to 350.
8. Cook for eight minutes

NUTRITION: Calories 150 Protein 13g Fat 9.6g Carbs 1.3g

Ham Hash

Basic Recipe

Preparation Time: 5 minutes **Cooking Time:** 20 minutes **Servings:** 4 **INGREDIENTS:**

- 5 ounces parmesan
- 10 ounces ham
- 1 teaspoon black pepper
- 1 teaspoon paprika
- 1 egg
- ½ onions
- 1 tablespoon butter

DIRECTIONS:

1. Start by shredding your parmesan, and then slice your ham into strips.
2. Peel your onion before dicing it, and then crack your egg open in a bowl. Whisk well, and then add in your butter, diced onions, and ham strips.
3. Sprinkle this mixture with paprika and black pepper.
4. Mix well, and heat your air fryer to 350.
5. Transfer this mixture into three separate ramekins, sprinkling with parmesan.
6. Make sure to preheat your air fryer, and cook for ten minutes Serve warm.

NUTRITION: Calories 372 Protein 33.2g Fat 23.7g Carbs 5.9g

Pork Fried Rice

Basic Recipe

Preparation Time: 5 minutes **Cooking Time:** 20 minutes **Servings:** 3 **INGREDIENTS:**

- 2 eggs
- 2 cloves garlic, chopped
- ½ cauliflower head, medium
- 3 green capsicums, mini
- 2 cups pork belly
- 2 onions
- 1 teaspoon black sesame seeds
- 1 teaspoon picked ginger
- 1 tablespoon soy sauce

DIRECTIONS:
1. Start by chopping your cauliflower to make small florets.
2. Get out a food processor, placing your cauliflower inside, and pulse until you get cauliflower rice.
3. Preheat your air fryer to 400, and then grease down your basket.
4. Beat your eggs, and then swirl them into your air fryer. Allow them to cook for five minutes, turning it down to 350.
5. Add in your cauliflower rice and pork next before tossing in your soy sauce and onion. Cook for another ten minutes at 375.
6. Garnish with picked ginger and sesame seeds.

NUTRITION: Calories 376 Protein 34 g Fat 33 g Carbs 9.6 g

Ketogenic Mac & Cheese

Basic Recipe

Preparation Time: 5 minutes **Cooking Time:** 20 minutes **Servings:** 4 **INGREDIENTS:**

- 3 tablespoons avocado oil
- Sea salt & black pepper to taste
- 1 cauliflower, medium
- ¼ cup heavy cream
- ¼ cup almond milk, unsweetened
- 1 cup cheddar cheese, shredded

DIRECTIONS:

1. Start by preheating your air fryer to 400, and then make sure to grease your air fryer basket.
2. Chop your cauliflower into florets, and then Drizzle with oil over them. Toss until they're well coated, and then season with salt and pepper to taste.
3. Heat your cheddar, heavy cream, milk and avocado oil in a pot, pouring the mixture over your cauliflower.
4. Cook for fourteen minutes, and then serve warm. **NUTRITION:** Calories 135.5 Protein 27 g Fat 10.2 g Carbs 1.4 g

Salmon Pie

Intermediate Recipe Preparation Time: 5 minutes **Cooking Time:** 45 minutes **Servings:** 8 **INGREDIENTS:**

- 1 teaspoon paprika
- ½ cup cream
- ½ teaspoons baking soda
- 1 ½ cups almond flour
- 1 onion, diced
- 1 tablespoon apple cider vinegar
- 1 lb. Salmon
- 1 tablespoon chives
- 1 teaspoon dill
- 1 teaspoon oregano
- 1 teaspoon butter
- 1 teaspoon parsley
- 1 egg

DIRECTIONS:

5. Start by beating your eggs in a bowl, making sure they're whisked well. Add in your cream, whisking for another two minutes
6. Add in your apple cider vinegar and baking soda, stirring well.
7. Add in your almond flour, combining until it makes a non-stick, smooth dough.
8. Chop your salmon into pieces, and then sprinkle your seasoning over it.
9. Mix well, and then cut your dough into two parts.
10. Place parchment paper over your air fryer basket tray, placing the first part of your dough in the tray to form a crust. Add in your salmon filling.
11. Roll out the second part, covering your salmon filling. Secure the edges, and then heat your air fryer to 360.
12. Cook for fifteen minutes, and then reduce the heat to 355, cooking for another fifteen minutes
13. Slice and serve warm.

NUTRITION: Calories 134 Protein 13.2 g Fat 8.1 g Carbs 2.2 g

Garlic Chicken Stir

Basic Recipe

Preparation Time: 5 minutes **Cooking Time:** 20 minutes **Servings:** 4 **INGREDIENTS:**

- ½ Cup coconut milk
- ½ cup chicken stock
- 2 tablespoons curry paste
- 1 tablespoon lemongrass
- 1 tablespoon apple cider vinegar
- 2 teaspoons garlic, minced
- 1 onion
- 1 lb. Chicken breast, skinless & boneless
- 1 teaspoon olive oil

DIRECTIONS:

1. Start by cubing your chicken, and then peel your onion before dicing it.
2. Combine your onion and chicken together in your air fryer basket, and then preheat it to 365. Cook for five minutes
3. Add in your garlic, apple cider vinegar, coconut milk, lemongrass, curry paste and chicken stock. Mix well, and cook for ten minutes more.
4. Stir well before serving.

NUTRITION: Calories 275 Protein 25.6 g Fat 15.7 g Carbs 5.9 g

Chicken Stew

Basic Recipe

Preparation Time: 5 minutes **Cooking Time:** 25 minutes **Servings:** 4 **INGREDIENTS:**

- 1 teaspoon cilantro
- 8 ounces chicken breast, boneless & skinless
- 1 onion
- ½ cup spinach
- 2 cups chicken stock
- 5 ounces cabbage
- 6 ounces cauliflower
- 1 teaspoon salt
- 1 green bell pepper
- 1/3 cup heavy cream
- 1 teaspoon paprika
- 1 teaspoon butter
- 1 teaspoon cayenne pepper

DIRECTIONS:

1. Start by cubing your chicken breast, and then sprinkling your cilantro, cayenne, salt and paprika over it.
2. Heat your air fryer to 365, and then melt your butter in your air fryer basket.
3. Add your chicken cubes in, cooking it for four minutes
4. Chop your spinach, and then dice your onion.
5. Shred your cabbage and cut your cauliflower into florets. Chop your green pepper next, and then add them into your air fryer.
6. Pour your chicken stock and heavy cream in, and then reduce your air fryer to 360. Cook for eight minutes, and stir before serving.

NUTRITION: Calories 102 Protein 9.8 g Fat 4.5 g Carbs 4.1 g

Goulash

Basic Recipe

Preparation Time: 5 minutes **Cooking Time:** 11 minutes **Serving:** 6 **INGREDIENTS:**

- 1 white onion
- 2 green peppers, chopped
- 1 teaspoon olive oil
- 14 ounces ground chicken
- 2 tomatoes
- ½ cup chicken stock
- 1 teaspoon sea salt, fine
- 2 cloves garlic, sliced
- 1 teaspoon black pepper
- 1 teaspoon mustard

DIRECTIONS:

1. Peel your onion before chopping it roughly.
2. Spray your air fryer down with olive oil before preheating it to 365.
3. Add in your chopped green pepper, cooking for five minutes
4. Add your ground chicken and cubed tomato next. Mix well, and cook for six minutes
5. Add in the chicken stock, salt, pepper, mustard and garlic. Mix well, and cook for six minutes more. Serve warm.

NUTRITION: Calories 161 Protein 20.3 g Fat 6.1 g Carbs 4.3 g

Beef & broccoli

Basic recipe

Preparation time: 5 minutes **Cooking time:** 20 minutes **Servings:** 4 **INGREDIENTS:**

- 1 teaspoon paprika
- 1 onion
- 1/3 cup water
- 6 ounces broccoli
- 10 ounces beef brisket
- 1 teaspoon canola oil
- 1 teaspoon butter
- ½ teaspoon chili flakes
- 1 tablespoon flax seeds

DIRECTIONS:

1. Start by chopping your beef brisket, and then sprinkle it with chili flakes and paprika. Mix your meat well, and then preheat your air fryer to 360.
2. Spray your air fryer down with canola oil, placing your beef in the basket tray. Cook for seven minutes, and make sure to stir once while cooking.
3. Chop your broccoli into florets, and then add them into your air fryer basket next.
4. Add in your butter and flax seeds before mixing in your water. Slice your onion, adding it into to, and stir well.
5. Cook at 265 for six minutes
6. Serve warm.

NUTRITION: Calories 187 Protein 23.4 g Fat 7.3 g Carbs 3.8 g

Ground Beef Mash

Basic Recipe

Preparation Time: 5 minutes **Cooking Time:** 20 minutes **Servings:** 4

INGREDIENTS:

- 1 lb. Ground beef
- 1 onion
- 1 teaspoon garlic, sliced
- ¼ cup cream
- 1 teaspoon white pepper
- 1 teaspoon olive oil
- 1 teaspoon dill
- 2 teaspoons chicken stock
- 2 green peppers
- 1 teaspoon cayenne pepper

DIRECTIONS:

1. Start by peeling your onion before grating it. Combine it with your sliced garlic, and then sprinkle your ground beef down with it. Add in your white pepper, and then add your cayenne and dill.
2. Coat your air fryer basket down with olive oil, heating it up to 365.
3. Place the spiced beef in the basket, cooking for three minutes before stirring. Add in the rest of your grated onion mixture and chicken stock, and then cook for two minutes more.
4. Chop your green peppers into small pieces, and then add them in.
5. Add in your cream, and stir well.
6. Allow it to cook for ten minutes more.
7. Mash your mixture to make sure it's scrambled before serving warm.

NUTRITION: Calories 258   Protein 35.5 G Fat 9.3 G Carbs 4.9 G

Chicken Casserole

Basic Recipe

Preparation Time: 5 minutes **Cooking Time:** 30 minutes **Servings:** 4 **INGREDIENTS:**

- 1 tablespoon butter
- 9 ounces round chicken
- ½ onion
- 5 ounces bacon
- Sea salt & black pepper to taste
- 1 teaspoon turmeric
- 1 teaspoon paprika
- 6 ounces cheddar cheese, shredded
- 1 egg
- ½ cup cream
- 1 tablespoon almond flour

DIRECTIONS:

1. Spread your butter into your air fryer tray, and then add in your ground chicken. Season it with salt and pepper, and then add in your turmeric and paprika. Stir well, and then add in your cheddar cheese.
2. Beat your egg into your ground chicken, and mix well. Whisk your cream and almond flour together.
3. Peel and dice your onion, and ten add it into your air fryer too.
4. Layer your cheese and bacon, and then heat your air fryer to 380. Cook for eighteen minutes, and then allow it to cool slightly before serving.

NUTRITION: Calories 396 Protein 30.4 g Fat 28.6 g Carbs 2.8 g

Chicken Hash

Basic Recipe

Preparation Time: 5 minutes **Cooking Time:** 20 minutes **Servings:** 3 **INGREDIENTS:**

- 1 Tablespoon Water
- 1 Green Pepper
- ½ Onion
- 6 Ounces Cauliflower
- Chicken Fillet, 7 Ounces
- 1 Tablespoon cream
- 3 Tablespoon Butter
- Black Pepper to taste

DIRECTIONS:

5. Start by roughly chopping your cauliflower before placing it in a blender. Blend until you get a cauliflower rice.
6. Chop your chicken into small pieces, and then get out your chicken fillets. Sprinkle with black pepper.
7. Heat your air fryer to 380, and then put your chicken in the air fryer basket. Add in your water and cream, cooking for six minutes
8. Reduce the heat to 360, and then dice your green pepper and onion.
9. Add this to your cauliflower rice, and then add in your butter. Mix well, and then add it to your chicken. Cook for eight minutes
10. Serve warm.

NUTRITION: Calories 261 Protein 21 g Fat 16.8 g Carbs 4.4 g

DINNER

Air Fried Chicken Tikkas

Basic Recipe

Preparation Time: 10 minutes **Cooking Time:** 15 minutes **Servings:** 4 **INGREDIENTS:**

For marinade:
- 1¼ pounds chicken, bones cut into small bite size
- ¼ pound cherry tomatoes
- 1 cup yogurt
- 1 tablespoon ginger garlic paste (fresh)
- 3 bell peppers, 1l cut size
- 2 tablespoons chili powder
- 2 tablespoons cumin powder
- 1 tablespoon turmeric powder
- 2 tablespoons coriander powder
- 1 teaspoon garam masala powder
- 2 teaspoons olive oil
- Salt – to taste For garnishing:
- 1 lemon, cut into half
- ⅓ cup Coriander, fresh, chopped
- 1 medium Onion, nicely sliced
- Mint leaves, fresh – few

DIRECTIONS:

1. In a large bowl mix all the marinade ingredients and coat it thoroughly on the chicken pieces.
2. Cover the bowl and set aside for 2 hours minimum. If you can refrigerate overnight, it can give better marinade effect.
3. Thread the chicken in the skewers along with bell peppers and tomatoes alternately.
4. Preheat your air fryer at 200 degrees Celsius.
5. Spread an aluminum liner on the air fryer basket and arrange the skewers on it.
6. Set the timer for 15 minutes and grill it.
7. Turn the skewer intermittently for an even grilling.
8. Once done, put into a plate and garnish with the given ingredients before serving.

NUTRITION: Calories 400 Fat 20g Carbs 17.4g Protein 46.9g

Air Fryer Cauliflower Rice

Basic Recipe

Preparation Time: 10 minutes **Cooking Time:** 20 minutes **Servings:** 3 **INGREDIENTS:**

- Segment - 1
- ½ firm tofu
- ½ cup onion, chopped
- 2 tablespoons low sodium soy sauce
- 1 cup carrot diced
- ½ teaspoon turmeric powder
- Segment – 2
- 3 cups cauliflower rice
- ½ cup frozen peas
- 2 tablespoons low sodium soy sauce
- 1½ teaspoons sesame oil, toasted
- 1 tablespoon rice vinegar
- 1 tablespoon ginger, grated
- ½ cup broccoli, finely chopped
- 2 cloves garlic, minced

DIRECTIONS:

1. Crumble tofu in a large bowl. Toss the crumbled tofu with sector 1 ingredients.
2. Set the air fryer temperature to 190 degree Celsius and cook for 10 minutes. Shake the air fryer basket 2-3 times during the cooking in progress.
3. In another large bowl, combine all the ingredients mentioned in the segment 2.
4. After 10 minutes of cooking, transfer the second segment ingredients over the cooked food. Shake the air basket tray and cook for 10 minutes at 190 degrees Celsius. Make sure to shake the air fryer basket intermittently for a better baking result. When the cauliflower rice becomes tender, it is ready to serve.
5. Serve hot along with your favorite sauce.

NUTRITION: Calories 126 Fat 5g Carbs 14g Protein 7.8g

Buttery Cod

Basic Recipe

Preparation Time: 5 minutes **Cooking Time:** 15 minutes **Servings:** 4 **INGREDIENTS:**

- 2 tbsp parsley, chopped
- 3 tbsp butter, melted
- 8 cherry tomatoes, halved
- 0.25 cup tomato sauce
- 2 cod fillets, cubed

DIRECTIONS:

1. Turn on the air fryer to 390 degrees.
2. Combine all of the ingredients and put them into a pan that works with the air fryer.
3. After 12 minutes of baking, you can divide this between the four bowls and enjoy.

NUTRITION: Calories 232 Fat 8g Carbs 5g Protein 11g

Creamy Chicken

Basic Recipe

Preparation Time: 5 minutes **Cooking Time:** 15 minutes **Servings:** 4 **INGREDIENTS:**

- Pepper and salt
- 1 tsp olive oil
- 1 0.5 tsp sweet paprika
- 0.25 cup coconut cream
- 4 chicken breasts, cubed

DIRECTIONS:

1. Turn on the air fryer to 370 degrees. Prepare a frying pan that fits into the machine with some oil before adding the ingredients inside. Add this to the air fryer and let it bake. After 17 minutes, you can divide between the few plates and serve!

NUTRITION: Calories 250 Fat 12g Carbs 5g Protein 11g

Mushroom and Turkey Stew

Basic Recipe

Preparation Time: 5 minutes **Cooking Time:** 25 minutes **Servings:** 4 **INGREDIENTS:**

- Pepper and salt
- 1 tbsp parsley, chopped
- 0.25 cup tomato sauce
- 1 turkey breast cubed
- 0.5 lb. Brown mushrooms, sliced

DIRECTIONS:

2. Turn on the air fryer to 350 degrees. Pick out a pan and mix the tomato sauce, pepper, salt, mushrooms, and turkey together. Add to the air fryer.
3. After 25 minutes, the stew is done—divides between four bowls and top with the parsley.

NUTRITION: Calories 220 Fat 12g Carbs 5g Protein 12g

Basil Chicken

Basic Recipe

Preparation Time: 5 minutes

Cooking Time: 15 minutes **Servings:** 4

INGREDIENTS:
- Pepper and salt
- 2 tsp smoked paprika
- 0.5 tsp dried basil
- 0.5 cup chicken stock
- 1 0.5 lb chicken breasts, cubed

DIRECTIONS:
4. Turn on the air fryer to 390 degrees.
5. Bring out a pan and toss the ingredients inside before putting it into the air fryer.
6. After 25 minutes of baking, divide this between a few plates and serve with a side salad.

NUTRITION: Calories 223 Fat 12g Carbs 5g Protein 13g

Eggplant Bake

Basic Recipe

Preparation Time: 5 minutes **Cooking Time:** 15 minutes **Servings:** 4 **INGREDIENTS:**

- 2 tsp olive oil
- Pepper and salt
- 4 spring onions, chopped
- 1 hot chili pepper, chopped
- 2 eggplants, cubed
- 4 garlic cloves, minced
- 0.5 cup cilantro, chopped
- 0.5 lb cherry tomatoes, cubed

DIRECTIONS:

7. Turn on the air fryer and let it heat up to 380 degrees.
8. Prepare a baking pan that will go into the air fryer and mix all of the ingredients onto it.
9. Place into the air fryer to cook. After 15 minutes, divide between four bowls and serve.

NUTRITION: Calories 232 Fat 12g Carbs 5g Protein 10g

Meatball Casserole

Basic Recipe

Preparation Time: 5 minutes **Cooking Time:** 15 minutes **Servings:** 6 **INGREDIENTS:**

- 1 tbsp thyme, chopped
- 0.25 cup parsley, chopped
- 0.33 lb turkey sausage
- 1 egg, beaten
- 0.66 lb ground beef
- 2 tbsp olive oil
- 1 shallot, minced
- 1 tbsp Dijon mustard
- 3 garlic cloves, minced
- 2 tbsp whole milk
- 1 tbsp rosemary, chopped

DIRECTIONS:

10. Turn on the air fryer to a High setting and then give it time to heat up with some oil inside.
11. Add the garlic and onions and cook for a few minutes to make soft.
12. Add the milk and bread crumbs to a bowl and then mix. Then add in the rest of the ingredients and set aside to soak.
13. Use this mixture, after five minutes, to prepare some small meatballs. Add these to the air fryer.
14. Turn the heat up to 400 degrees to cook. After 10 minutes, take the lid off and shake the basket. Cook another five minutes before serving.

NUTRITION: Calories 168 Fat 11g Carbs 4g Protein 12g

Herbed Lamb Rack

Basic Recipe

Preparation Time: 5 minutes **Cooking Time:** 10 minutes **Servings:** 2 **INGREDIENTS:**

- 4 tbsp olive oil
- 0.5 tsp pepper
- 1 tbsp dried thyme
- 2 tbsp dried rosemary
- 0.5 tsp salt
- 2 tsp garlic, minced
- 1 lb rack of lamb

DIRECTIONS:

15. Turn on the air fryer to 400 degrees. In a bowl, combine the herbs and olive oil well.
16. Use this to coat the lamb before adding to the basket of the air fryer.
17. Close the lid, and then let this cook. Halfway through, you can shake the basket to make sure nothing sticks.
18. After ten minutes, take the lamb out and enjoy.

NUTRITION: Calories 542 Fat 37g Carbs 3g Protein 45g

Baked Beef

Intermediate Recipe Preparation Time: 10 minutes **Cooking Time:** 60minutes **Servings:** 5

INGREDIENTS:
- 1 bunch garlic cloves
- 1 bunch fresh herbs, mixed
- 2 sliced onions
- Olive oil
- 3 lbs beef
- 2 celery sticks, chopped
- 2 carrots, chopped

DIRECTIONS:
19. Great up a pan and then add the herbs, olive oil, beef roast, and vegetables inside.
20. Turn the air fryer on to 400 degrees and place the pan inside. Let this heat up and close the lid.
21. After an hour of cooking, open the lid and then serve this right away.

NUTRITION: Calories 306 Fat 21g Carbs 10g Protein 32g

Old-Fashioned Pork Chops

Basic Recipe

Preparation Time: 5 minutes **Cooking Time:** 15 minutes **Servings:** 6 **INGREDIENTS:**

- Salt
- 0.5 tsp onion powder
- 0.25 tsp chili powder
- 0.25 tsp. Pepper
- 1 tsp smoked paprika
- 1 cup pork rind
- 3 tbsp parmesan, grated
- 5 boneless pork chops
- 2 beaten eggs

DIRECTIONS:

22. Use the pepper and salt to season the pork chops. Blend the rind to make some crumbs.
23. In another bowl, beat the eggs and then coat this onto the pork chops with the crumbs.
24. Take out the air fryer and set it to 400 degrees to heat up.
25. When this is done, add the pork chops into the air fryer and let it heat up. When this is halfway done, flip the pork chops over and cook a little more.
26. After 15 minutes of cooking, turn off the air fryer and serve.

NUTRITION: Calories 391 Fat 18g Carbs 17g Protein 38g

Turkey Pillows

Basic Recipe

Preparation Time: 5 minutes **Cooking Time:** 10 minutes **Servings:** 4 **INGREDIENTS:**

- 15 slices turkey breast
- 2 jars Cream cheese
- 1 Egg yolk
- 4 cups Flour
- 20.5 tbsp Dried granular yeast
- 2 tbsp Sugar
- 10.75 tsp Salt
- 0.25 cup Olive oil
- 0.33 cup Water
- 1 cup Milk with an egg inside

DIRECTIONS:

27. Mix the ingredients for the dough with your hands until smooth. Make it into small balls and put on a floured surface. Open the dough balls with a roller to make it square. Cut into small pieces. Fill with the turkey breast and a bit of cream cheese. Close the points together.
28. Turn on the air fryer to 400 degrees. Place a few of the balls inside and let them cook. After five minutes, take these out and repeat with the rest of the pillows until done.

NUTRITION: Calories 528 Fat 30g Carbs 23g Protein 44g

Chicken Wings

Basic Recipe

Preparation Time: 5 minutes **Cooking Time:** 25 minutes **Servings:** 2 **INGREDIENTS:**

- 2 tbsp chives
- 0.5 tbsp salt
- 1 tbsp lime
- 0.5 tbsp ginger, chopped
- 1 tbsp garlic, minced
- 1 tbsp chili paste
- 2 tbsp honey
- 0.5 tbsp cornstarch
- 1 tbsp soy sauce
- Oil
- 10 chicken wings

DIRECTIONS:

29. Dry the chicken and then cover it with spray. Add into the air fryer that is preheated to 400 degrees.
30. Let this cook for a bit. During that time, add the rest of the ingredients to a bowl and set aside.
31. After 25 minutes, the chicken is done. Add the chicken into a bowl and top with the sauce. Sprinkle the chives on top and serve.

NUTRITION: Calories 81 Fat 5g Carbs 0g Protein 8g

Chicken Cordon Bleu

Basic Recipe

Preparation Time: 5 minutes **Cooking Time:** 40 minutes **Servings:** 6 **INGREDIENTS:**

- Garlic clove (1, chopped)
- Eggs (2)
- Butter (2 tsps., melted)
- Bread (1 c., ground)
- Flour (0.25 c.)
- Fresh thyme (2 tsps.)
- Swiss cheese (16 slices)
- Ham (8 slices)
- Chicken breasts (4)

DIRECTIONS:

1. Turn on the air fryer to heat to 350 degrees.
2. Flatten out the chicken and then fill with two slices of cheese, ham, and then cheese again. Roll up and use a toothpick to keep together.
3. Mix the garlic, thyme, and bread together with the butter. Beat the eggs and season the flour with pepper and salt.
4. Pass the chicken rolls through the flour, then the egg, and then the breadcrumbs. Add to the air fryer to cook.
5. After 20 minutes, take the chicken out and cool down before serving.

NUTRITION: Calories 387 Fat 20g Carbs 18g Protein 33g

Fried Chicken

Basic Recipe

Preparation Time: 5 minutes **Cooking Time:** 25 minutes **Servings:** 4 **INGREDIENTS:**

- Lemon (1)
- Ginger (1, grated)
- Ground pepper, salt, and garlic powder
- Chopped chicken (1 lb.)

DIRECTIONS:

1. Add the chicken to a bowl with the rest of the ingredients. Let it set for a bit to marinate.
2. After 15 minutes, add some oil to the air fryer and let it heat up to 320 degrees.
3. Add the chicken inside to cook for 25 minutes, shaking it a few times to cook through. Serve warm.

NUTRITION: Calories 345 Fat 3g Carbs 23g Protein 3g

Sesame Chicken

Basic Recipe

Preparation Time: 5 minutes **Cooking Time:** 50minutes **Servings:** 4 **INGREDIENTS:**

- Soy sauce
- Pepper
- Salt
- Olive oil
- Breadcrumbs
- Egg
- 1 lb. Chicken breast

DIRECTIONS:

1. Slice the chicken into fillets and add to the bowl with the sesame and soy sauce. Let this marinate for half an hour. Beat the eggs and then pass the chicken through it.
2. Add to the grill of the air fryer at 350 degrees. Let it grill for a bit.
3. After 20 minutes, take the chicken off and let it cool down before serving.

NUTRITION: Calories 375 Fat 18g Carbs 6g Protein 35g

Chicken and Potatoes

Basic Recipe

Preparation Time: 5 minutes **Cooking Time:** 55minutes **Servings:** 2 **INGREDIENTS:**

- Pepper and salt
- Provencal herbs
- 2 Chicken pieces
- 4 Potatoes
- Olive oil

DIRECTIONS:

4. Peel the skin from the potatoes and cut into slices. Add some pepper and place into the air fryer.
5. Preheat to 340 degrees. Cover the chicken with the herbs, pepper, salt, and oil and add it in with the potatoes.
6. Cook this until well done. After forty minutes, turn the chicken around and let it cook another 15 minutes before serving.

NUTRITION: Calories 200 Fat 4g Carbs 18g Protein 22g

Polish Sausage and Sourdough Kabobs

Basic Recipe

Preparation Time: 5 minutes **Cooking Time:** 15 minutes **Servings:** 4 **INGREDIENTS:**

- 1 pound smoked Polish beef sausage, sliced
- 1 tablespoon mustard
- 1 tablespoon olive oil
- 2 tablespoons Worcestershire sauce
- 2 bell peppers, sliced
- 2 cups sourdough bread, cubed
- Salt and ground black pepper, to taste

DIRECTIONS:

7. Toss the sausage with the mustard, olive, and Worcestershire sauce. Thread sausage, peppers, and bread onto skewers.
8. Sprinkle with salt and black pepper.
9. Cook in the preheated Air Fryer at 360 degrees F for 11 minutes Brush the skewers with the reserved marinade. Bon appétit!

NUTRITION: Calories 284 Fat 13.8g Carbs 16.5g Protein 23.1g

Ranch Meatloaf with Peppers

Basic Recipe

Preparation Time: 5 minutes **Cooking Time:** 30 minutes **Servings:** 5 **INGREDIENTS:**

- 1 pound beef, ground
- 1/2 pound veal, ground
- 1 egg
- 4 tablespoons vegetable juice
- 1 cup crackers, crushed
- 2 bell peppers, chopped
- 1 onion, chopped
- 2 garlic cloves, minced
- 2 tablespoons tomato paste
- 2 tablespoons soy sauce
- 1 (1-ounce) package ranch dressing mix
- Sea salt, to taste
- 1/2 teaspoon ground black pepper, to taste
- 7 ounces tomato paste
- 1 tablespoon Dijon mustard

DIRECTIONS:

1. Start by preheating your Air Fryer to 330 degrees F.
2. In a mixing bowl, thoroughly combine the ground beef, veal, egg, vegetable juice, crackers, bell peppers, onion, garlic, tomato paste, and soy sauce, ranch dressing mix, salt, and ground black pepper. Mix until everything is well incorporated and press into a lightly greased meatloaf pan.
3. Cook approximately 25 minutes in the preheated Air Fryer. Whisk the tomato paste with the mustard and spread the topping over the top of your meatloaf.
4. Continue to cook 2 minutes more. Let it stand on a cooling rack for 6 minutes before slicing and serving. Enjoy!

NUTRITION: Calories 411 Fat 31.4g Carbs 10g Protein 28.2g

Indian Beef Samosas

Basic Recipe

Preparation Time: 5 minutes **Cooking Time:** 30 minutes **Servings:** 8 **INGREDIENTS:**

- 1 tablespoon sesame oil
- 4 tablespoons shallots, minced
- 2 cloves garlic, minced
- 2 tablespoons green chili peppers, chopped
- 1/2 pound ground chuck
- 4 ounces bacon, chopped
- Salt and ground black pepper, to taste
- 1 teaspoon cumin powder
- 1 teaspoon turmeric
- 1 teaspoon coriander
- 1 cup frozen peas, thawed
- 1 (16-ounce) of phyllo dough
- 1 egg, beaten with 2 tablespoons of water (egg wash)

DIRECTIONS:

10. Heat the oil in a saucepan over medium-high heat. Once hot, sauté the shallots, garlic, and chili peppers until tender, about 3 minutes
11. Then, add the beef and bacon; continue to sauté an additional 4 minutes, crumbling with a fork. Season it with salt, pepper, cumin powder, turmeric, and coriander. Stir in peas.
12. Then, preheat your Air Fryer to 330 degrees F. Brush the Air Fryer basket with cooking oil.
13. Place 1 to 2 tablespoons of the mixture onto each phyllo sheet. Fold the sheets into triangles, pressing the edges. Brush the tops with egg wash.
14. Bake it for 7 to 8 minutes, working with batches. Serve with Indian tomato sauce if desired. Enjoy!

NUTRITION: Calories 266 Fat 13g Carbs 24.5g Protein 12.2g

CPSIA information can be obtained
at www.ICGtesting.com
Printed in the USA
BVHW040713220321
603170BV00004B/760

9 781802 144727